HURRICANE IRMA

Through My Eyes

Amia Wheatley

ACKNOWLEDGEMENTS

I would like to acknowledge the Almighty God; my creator, father, best friend, who continuously opens doors for me and keeps me growing; desiring more of Him.

To my parents Claudius and Alfreda Wheatley, my biggest supporters, I say thank you for pushing me.

To my apostle Curnal P. Fahie, thank you for always encouraging me.

To my grandmother Delphina Wattley, you kept me entertained with old time games and stories that I love during the months of no electricity; thank you.

To my aunt and her husband, Andrea and Ancel Bowen; thank you. You guys made the best meals during the entire time we spent together after the storm.

To my uncle Derrick Gordon, it was reassuring to know that we had a place to go if we needed to leave. All of this could not be possible without your help and I am forever grateful.

A big shout out to my Graphic designer, artist, producer Joycelyn Garcia of Diamond Designz. You made me look good and made my work come alive. Keep up this level of excellence.

Not forgetting other family members and my friends whose names are too numerous to mention; a heartfelt thank you to all of you.

FOREWORD BY APOSTLE CURNAL P. FAHIE

It gives me great pleasure to write this foreword. I just finished reading "Hurricane Irma Through My Eyes". I did it in one sitting, not only because it's short but because it was exciting, engaging, energizing, entertaining, emotional and full of empathy!

From the first sentence, Amia pulls you into her 10-year-old world and captivates your mind. Then she is relentless in her pursuit to make you relive the trauma of Irma with her. By the end of her story, you would have certainly experienced Irma through her eyes, and like her, decide that you don't want to endure that again.

Amia, I'm so extraordinarily and ecstatically proud of you! My years of preaching, pushing, pulling and prodding for the people (adult and youth alike) to push beyond the norm, and be all that they can be, is not in vain.

The best is still yet to come in your life in Jesus' Name. There are more manuscripts to write, products to invent, songs to compose, dances to choreograph and educational hurdles to conquer. The Conqueror lives in you so go and occupy till He comes in Jesus' Name (Lk19:13).

Amia, always remember that you are a walking, talking, breathing, moving solution/answer to a problem that the world has.

I decree and declare that you are smarter than your teachers, more clever than the ancient, and wiser than the men of old (Ps 119:99-100). Let the good Hand of the Lord be upon you, like it was on Joshua to grant him good success and on Nehemiah to grant him supernatural favour. I prophecy that you will go further than your forefathers. I command the earth and its atmosphere to adjust to receive the gift of God in you (Josh 1:5-9; Neh 2:18).

Don't you dare dimmin' your light so that others may feel bright. May the light of Jesus in your life illuminate your part as you light the sphere over which He gives you influence/dominion.

Beloved, this book is a must read! I highly recommend it to you and yours.

TABLE OF CONTENTS

1

CHAPTER ONE

"A hurricane was coming"; the words heard over the radio, on the internet, on the TV and by the adults all around. But what really was a hurricane? I didn't understand it then. I was use to sunny-clear skies and crystal-clear waters. I was accustomed to fun days at the park with my friends and siblings. I was use to riding my bike! I was not accustomed to hurricanes!

I had just celebrated my 10th birthday and my little brother his 6th in August. We celebrated a few days before with family and friends. My parents gave my brother the best party a 6-year-old could ever have, the Saturday before Irma came. I didn't have a big party like him because the year before, a big party was thrown for me as I turned 9. Then, as if my brother's birthday and mine never happened, we began to prepare for the hurricane.

Some of the adults were boarding up the windows and doors. They were cleaning their surroundings, and carrying useless, loose items, which were unnecessary missiles from their yard to the garbage dump.

Even though I saw them doing these things, I still didn't quite understand why. No amount of preparation, however, could have prepared anyone for what was about to come.

2
CHAPTER TWO

The wind blew violently at the very top of the hill where we lived. Our doors had already begun to rock back and forth. It's at that very moment mom and dad began to prepare. I started to feel afraid and I could see in their eyes that they were also uncertain as to what would happen.

The last thing I remembered was, my mom sending my bigger brother to stay by my grandma until the storm was over because she lived alone. She also spoke to my uncle on the phone, updating him on all the things which were happening before it all began.

The strong wind suddenly knocked the phone line out. My parents could no longer make any calls. That's when it became serious; it suddenly became real!

3
CHAPTER THREE

My father grabbed a big strap and used it to attach the living room door to the living room closet. He held on to it while my mother asked me to help her push against the windows in my bedroom.

My windows would not stop dancing, and it seemed as if we were being overpowered by them. The wind pushed so hard against them that they felt as if they would have knocked us over. We got soaked from head to toe from the rain which came inside through the windows that we pushed against. We could not stop holding the windows to mop or to move anything from inside of the room because we feared they would have blown in.

I was so scared. I thought we would die. My hands were so sore pushing against the windows, I wanted to give up. It felt like we were pushing for hours. My mom was complaining about her ears feeling like they were going to pop all while she prayed through the entire ordeal.

Every now and again, my dad yelled out to us asking if we were okay. The noise surrounding us was so loud that he had to shout for us to hear him from inside of the room. My little brother was placed in a corner, in front of the bathroom door, just in case the door was flung open on my dad, or the windows on us. Dad said if it did, he would try to run, grab him and get to us so we could all head inside of the bathroom. That thought really scared me!

4

CHAPTER FOUR

The raging wind lasted about thirty minutes and then there was a calm. We were now inside of what was called the eye of the hurricane. It was calm for a moment, but nothing prepared us for what we were about to see. It was a total disaster. I felt sick to my stomach. Mom and dad looked worried. We wondered about my elderly grandparents who were located next door to us and my brother and grandma who were a few miles away from us.

As the eye of the hurricane moved away, the wind began to howl just as it did before. I tried to look outside to see what was happening but all I could see was white. Then it all made sense;

our location! We lived on the very top of the hill, and the Marina was below us. We saw white because of the water from the inlet. The wind spun so vigorously and as a result, the water spun which prevented me from seeing outside of the big windows in my room.

5
CHAPTER FIVE

After what seemed like a very long time, it was finally over. It took us two days to clear the debris which were thrown across our yard and to get out of our gap. It became a village effort. We had to work together even if we never did before. Neighbours became friends and we began to live like what was described to us in school as "back in the day".

We had no electricity, so my mom corned every piece of meat we had with lots of salt and hung them to dry. I remember seeing my mom prepare meals daily; everyone in the building got fed. During that time, when we were getting rid of debris from our yard, a rock fell on my foot and left a mark that is still there today. Whenever I would see that mark, I would suddenly remember how afraid I was.

6

CHAPTER SIX

Many fallen trees and objects were blocking what use to be our road. We worked tirelessly until the path was clear enough for us to walk down the hill and hopefully reach my brother and grandma who lived on the other side of the island from where we lived.

What would normally take fifteen minutes of driving to get to grandma's house, took over an hour. It was a scary feeling of uncertainty, but we had to know how grandma and my brother were.

On the way to grandma's house, we got to see that it was not only our side of the island that suffered tremendous loss, but all over the island. We walked and hiked to get to grandma's house. We climbed over and under several humongous trees that fell during the aftermath until we were finally close to grandma's house. My heart began to race. I then realized that by her was just as damaged as by us. However, grandma and my brother were safe. I can't say the same for the entire home, but we were thankful.

Tears of joy filled my eyes. My dad asked my grandma and brother to pack a bag and come with us. We did not care that we had no electricity; we were just glad that all of us had survived. We were all alive and we were grateful.

7
CHAPTER SEVEN

I hope that I never have to go through a storm of that sort in my lifetime ever again but if I do, I prefer to weather it with God's help.

One advantage I must say that I enjoyed after the storm was being able to see the big army jets that came in. We have an unobstructed view of the airport runway and so we used our binoculars to look at the jets coming in and leaving daily. It was a sight to see!

I will never forget what Hurricane Irma did to us and the British Virgin Islands, but I'm most grateful to still be alive with my family and friends.

-End-

PICTURES OF SOME OF THE DESTRUCTION HURRICANE IRMA CAUSED